Doggie Doodles

Coloring Book

Angela González
Illustration, design and texts

Dedicate to my family

This Book Belongs to:

....

Angela González, Lala, was born in Medellín, Colombia. Since she was little she remembers having a very particular taste for drawing and illustration. Lala studied Graphic Design and then drawing and oil painting. Lala´s talent and perseverance have enabled her to work in the fields of illustration and art, where she has captured a colorful, magical, and Naïve art movement style, playing with her images to represent the most beautiful scenes of her own fairytales. Colombia has always been Lala´s source of inspiration, its culture, folklore, landscapes and flowers are reflected in her work, a country that is definitely for her a wonderland.

Made in United States
Troutdale, OR
06/18/2024

20636680R00066